I Still Deserve It.

Affirmations for women
who refuse to give up on love.

Derrick Jaxn

Printed in the United States of America

First Printing, 2017
ISBN: 978-0-9910336-4-5
Shop Derrick Jaxn LLC

www.shopderrickjaxn.com

contactshopderrickjaxn@gmail.com

TABLE OF CONTENTS

Everywhere we turn, there are messages being sent to our subconscious. Whether they come in the form of social media, conversations with our peers, or firsthand experiences, many of those messages corrode our hope in obtaining true happiness the older we get. However, the messages we are sent will never be more significant than the messages we embrace. That's what determines how our soul will grow or deteriorate over our lifetime.

The importance to not only block out empty, negative messages but also filter the ones that find their way into our system by rinsing ourselves daily in positive affirmations cannot be overstated. If we do not shape our minds, someone, everyone, and everything else will.

My desire is that this book will serve as seeds for your soul, and through daily repetition or even memorization, it will allow your happiness and mental health to blossom, particularly in your preparation for your soul mate. This book is not for simply reading, but for digesting, internalizing, and applying. It's time to give yourself the love you've always given so freely to everyone else. You still deserve it.

CHAPTER 1

If he's worth it, he'll wait.

I can't make him see me for who I am and the time I need to repair my heart. I can't make him accept me for the process I need to heal. But if he's worth it, he'll see that I am also worth it, and he will wait however long it takes to find my heart because he'll value it too much to give up so easily. I deserve a man who has patience for what he wants instead of settles for what's convenient.

CHAPTER 2

I will not break.

So many have come my way with ulterior motives and hidden agendas. Some have changed into completely different people; others were never good for me to begin with and revealed that as time went on. Either way, their destructive intentions have nothing to do with my worthiness of real love. I cannot control what I attract, but I will control what I accept, and I will use each learned lesson as my guide in doing so going forward. I give myself permission to make the mistake of trusting the wrong people and acknowledge my power to keep it from making me bitter.

Chapter 3

I'm beautiful, no compliments needed.

I love me, flaws and faults included. While I will graciously accept those who feel the same, it won't be necessary to validate that truth. My skin comes in the very tone God intended; my height was meant to be no higher or lower; and my curves were perfectly set to my predetermined design. I don't need to be anyone else to be beautiful, and I won't try to be in an effort to accept myself. I accept, appreciate, and love me just the way I am. Fully clothed, or completely bare, I am beautiful.

CHAPTER 4

The blessing was in their blindness.

I don't have to have answers as to why they didn't see in me what I see in myself to know they missed out. Their ignorance is not my burden. I refuse to weigh myself down with their missed opportunity to have the love I'm capable of giving. I know it's a blessing for those whose soul is blind to what's real to weed themselves out one way or another, to make room for a man whose eyes are wide open.

CHAPTER 5

The time for love may be later, but the time to love myself is right now.

I won't waste another moment waiting for secondhand love. I will create in me what will be multiplied later by the one I'll spend my life with instead of being dormant in the time being. I will invest in myself the same effort I expect from my future husband. Every day, second, and hour will be an ongoing upgrade for my heart, mind, body, and finances. Others will see my light shine and be inspired to do the same. I will feel no remorse or shame for turning my love inward until I'm found by the one worth sharing it with.

CHAPTER 6

I won't live with regrets from having an open heart.

I did my part by opening my heart. They did their damage by coming in with no intentions of staying. But damage can be undone, no matter how long it takes to do so. My open heart is a blessing when so many have theirs closed even though it has felt like a curse at times I let the wrong ones enter. I will not let that pain change me. I will not let their character flaws alter my path. My open heart is perfect for the open heart that will invite me, and I will not let those who didn't deserve me take that away.

CHAPTER 7

My all will be plenty for the right person.

It wouldn't have mattered if I sexed him more, fed him better, or looked any different. He didn't break my heart because of anything I did wrong. He broke it because his hands weren't made to hold it to begin with. I will judge more carefully and patiently the next time, and I will not hold back when the right man comes because neither will he.

CHAPTER 8

I will stop doubting my intuition.

I will not let this generation's lowered standards warp the way I view myself. I cannot let a ticking clock coerce me into knowingly wasting time. I will trust my intuition when it conflicts with their words so that I'm protected at all times. The confidence I have in my common sense is no accident no matter what they say to convince me otherwise. I have been through too much to keep repeating the same mistakes, and I do not feel bad for refusing to do so.

CHAPTER 9

I have the right to be selfish.

I've given so much to everyone else. I've stretched myself thin trying to help anyone I could. However, I have no responsibility to leave myself hanging to love others. Being my own priority is a necessity to be helpful to anyone else, and anyone who doesn't understand doesn't deserve my help. I will be selfish if it means saving me, without apology.

CHAPTER 10

He will put in the work.

If it means phone calls instead of texts, real date nights instead of "let's chill", or planning ahead instead of random pop-ups, he will do it. If he's smart enough and chosen just for me, he will do it. I am worth the effort and will accept nothing less even if a majority of others do.

CHAPTER 11

There's one man for me who will prove they are not all the same.

It will be in the way he looks at me, holds me, treats me, stays consistent, holds himself accountable, loves his mother, values family, and works towards his dreams while keeping me a priority. There is a man who will, despite his imperfections, have worked on himself enough so that he comes ready to love me. His lust won't compromise his loyalty. He will give me his heart, not excuses. He'll choose an opportunity for a lifetime with me over night after night with random women. He will find me, and he will show me why he was worth the time I waited for him.

CHAPTER 12

I'm worth another try.

I made bad decisions, but I won't dwell on them. I fell for BS a few times, but I will stand up again. I gave my trust and it was broken, but I will repair it and be more careful next time. While there is breath in my body, there is a chance to have exactly what I believe in. Millions find their forever-mate every single day, mine will come soon, and I will be ready when he does.

CHAPTER 13

I was equipped with the resilience necessary to come out on top.

They thought I couldn't make it without them. They thought I'd be lost and unhappy if they ever left. But they were wrong. They didn't know any better. They didn't realize that no matter how badly they hurt me, I would bounce back better than before. I've weathered those storms, kept my faith, held my head up high, and returned my crown back to itself rightful place. I will never allow it to be knocked off again.

CHAPTER 14

I will not run back, I will run forward.

While the temptation is there, I will follow my intelligence this time. I will not take my vivid memory for granted or push aside what I felt the last time I let my guard down for them. I will make it impossible to hurt me this time by locking them out since they've already shown me they don't deserve what's inside. I'm too valuable to continue being robbed of my trust, and I will not run back to the hands that hurt me. I will run forward, taking my dignity and sanity with me towards the happiness I never found with them.

CHAPTER 15

My past does not define me.

I've been hurt and I've done some hurting. I've made bad decisions and I've fallen for some tricks. But whatever has happened before this very moment is far less significant than what I do now. I don't have to be bound to the past when the future holds opportunity to know and do better. I can live free of any shame for being a human who still has much to learn, and no matter how far from perfect I am, I deserve to be loved.

CHAPTER 16

I didn't change, I grew.

O nce I saw what I didn't see before, I had to move accordingly. I was vulnerable for too long and was only leaving myself open to be harmed and I love myself too much to let that happen when I can do something to change it. I don't care how others view me; as long as I'm doing what's best for me, I'm not wrong. I'll lose whomever I have to in order to protect myself, and I will not apologize for it. If they really want to be in my life, they'll do what's necessary to deserve to be in it. Otherwise, I must take the necessary actions to ensure I never stop growing into who I'm destined to become.

CHAPTER 17

*My "Mr. Right" exists, even if he's not
here right now.*

The world waited billions of years to finally get me. I can wait a few more for the man who will too. A moment with him will outweigh all the moments it took to get to him. I won't keep my plate full of those who are not ready for what I have to offer even if it isn't always fun. My soul mate will be all the fun I could ever ask for, and I won't risk passing on that to keep entertaining what's currently being offered.

CHAPTER 18

*Every mistake I've made has gotten me closer
to my destiny.*

I make mistakes because I'm human. I don't always know how things will play out. But I do know that no matter what, I'm growing smarter and stronger by the day. I'm not the woman I was yesterday, and tomorrow I will be even better. I don't have to feel bad for doing exactly what I was designed to do: living, learning, and being a work in progress. The one I will grow old with is taking the same journey now so we can end our journey together.

CHAPTER 19

I reject all things that aim to degrade me.

My energy is too precious to pollute it with negative self-talk, outside opinions, empty critique, misleading thoughts, and manipulative perspectives. I will not indulge in spaces where I am not celebrated because there is too much to love about me to let anyone else turn my focus to things they feel are wrong about me. I have too much to be thankful for to ignore it so that I may seem unbiased. Loving myself too much to subject myself to destructive efforts is not bias, it is a necessity.

CHAPTER 20

He's saving himself so he can invest in me.

He's being called names, yet being unmoved by them. He's missing out on all the fun, while being completely fine with that. He's staying focused on things that will add value to us while sacrificing things that would only serve himself. He's letting himself heal, so my hurt will be a thing of the past. He's preserving his love for a woman like me who has everything I come with, and once he finds me, he'll be mine and only mine forever.

CHAPTER 21

My family goals are real and so is a man who shares them.

The children I will raise are as much of a goal for my future husband as they are me. The financial stability I'm working to create will be a shared effort by us as well. I can have everything I currently want because despite the majority of today's men who want only what's temporary, there are men who know the value of something real and most importantly, one woman like me to build that with.

CHAPTER 22

Distractions will not deter me.

Sometimes diversions from my path will be attractive, but I will not let it take me off course from my destiny. Some will have tempting offers that come short of what I'm after. Others will tell me that what I'm after is unreasonable, and I will accept none of them. I will hold firm to what I believe in, the same way my future husband is holding firm to the fact that I do exist. I am good at recognizing distractions, but I'm even better at steering clear from them.

CHAPTER 23

*Money is nice, love is even better, but I will not be forced
to choose between the two.*

An empire constructed by the hands of my husband and me is in my future. Others will ask how I became so lucky and my response will be that I'm not lucky. I worked on my own until I could combine it with his, and stopped entertaining those who only used me with nothing to offer. I will be found by a man who can balance his love for me and his ambition for financial security, and our children will inherit the fruits of our labor.

CHAPTER 24

I am not a victim, I am a victor.

Over the years, I've experienced more things than I've ever told anyone. I've had to deal with drama and snakes, lies and fakes, and everything in between. I've been underappreciated and overworked for everything I have now, but I am not a victim. I do not look for sympathy. I earn my respect, and will stand for nothing less than that. I find a way when there seems to be no way due to my determination. My work ethic warrants more than what I have, but I will one day have everything I want and more. The fact that I'm still standing here today is proof that I am truly a victor.

CHAPTER 25

Those who hate to see me win will one day have no other choice.

Good things come to those who wait, and better things come to those who work. I've done both. I've persevered against all odds. I've beaten "bad luck" and made it through what seemed to be impossible circumstances because I have what it takes to win. Those who lined up to see me fail will inadvertently witness me claim victory instead, and I will enjoy every second of it.

CHAPTER 26

There are many people I'll never know about who genuinely support and love me.

The same way I'm inspired by people I've never met or taken the opportunity to tell that I am, there are several people who absolutely love me. I make them proud with every accomplishment. I brighten their day with my energy and motivate them to be better versions of themselves. Through my own perseverance, they are convinced that a better tomorrow is possible if they, too, keep going.

CHAPTER 27

Not having my way hasn't always felt good, but it's been good for me.

At times, I've needed saving from myself. I didn't understand that before, but I can see that if every person I tried to love was still in my life, I would be much worse off. I would still be blind to their motives, still believing in their potential, and still fighting alone for a relationship that was never meant to be. The best thing to ever happen to me was being moved out of my own way, and because of that, my best is yet to come.

CHAPTER 28

I'm rightfully disappointed and dissatisfied.

If I was happy with the little that's been presented to me in the form of love interests, I would have canceled my chances for the most love has to offer. If I settled for what was in front of me, I wouldn't already be on my way to what's ahead. The best decisions I've ever made were to keep walking past those who were offering the bare minimum so that I can one day have the man who will give me his all and more to keep me in his life. Those were not mistakes, those were moments of tough self-love.

CHAPTER 29

My tears were not in vain.

I have no reason to be ashamed of the pain I've felt, for it proved I was human. I realize that it only molded me into the woman my future husband will be thankful for. My tears I've shed are what I will use to teach my daughter about how she is to be loved correctly, and my son about how he is to love fully. I will use my experiences as the guidance they need to avoid what I've endured, and they will be better because of it, the same way I am.

CHAPTER 30

One day, a man will appreciate everything about me that's been taken for granted.

I deserve to be looked at in my weakest moments as the one who keeps a man strong. My feelings deserve to be regarded highly instead of dismissed as "nagging". When I don't feel so pretty, I deserve to be reminded that I am in the eyes of my soul mate. I deserve to feel comfortable in all of my flaws, the same way I will make my husband feel about his. Only those undeserving of me will run away. The one meant for me will be happy to stay.

CHAPTER 31

My "baggage" will be viewed as my stripes by a man who appreciates a survivor.

While some men have fears of a woman with experience, who's had to learn things the hard way, whose guard is higher than normal due to being hurt in the past, there is a man for me who knows that a woman like that tends to be one of the best. He will see me and all of my scars, and promise not to cause another with actions that follow. He will touch me gently so that I'm comforted by his presence instead of leaving me with his absence once he realizes I'm not beautiful. The right man will see the heart I've locked away for that special someone and know that there must be something precious in it for me to hold it to me so closely, and he will pursue it with all of his might.

CHAPTER 32

I'm not crazy for wanting what this generation no longer values.

I want a home, not just a house. I want a family, not just kids. I want marriage, not just a boyfriend. Everything I want is also being yearned for by a man designated for me, and even if it takes time for us to get to that point, we will one day have exactly what our hearts desire.

CHAPTER 33

I forgive those who've done me wrong, but I won't forget what they've done.

No, I didn't get the apology I deserve, but I will give myself the peace of mind I'm long overdue. I can't change their hearts and make them pure, but I can protect my own from the inside out and prevent what they've done to me from making me bitter while remembering what they did so I'll never again be so naive. I will not carry the burden of hatred nor will I seek revenge, but I will build more meaningful and long-lasting relationships in the future based on what I've learned the painful way, and I will be happier as a result.

CHAPTER 34

Pain is temporary. Happiness is on the way.

I will not let myself define my life by this moment, no matter how easy it may be to do so. I will look forward to tomorrow and realize it's another chance to get it right despite how many times I've gotten it wrong. I was built for this journey, and even though it may get difficult, I know the destination will be well worth the ride.

CHAPTER 35

*I hold my head high because that's where my
standards are.*

I've worked too hard, held on too long, kept my faith too strong, and overcome too much to walk around with my head down. Out of admiration for myself, I will walk around today and every day like the champion I am. I will pull my shoulders back, keep my chin up, and smile even if it's difficult to because many have sacrificed for my opportunity to do so and I've been through much worse. It didn't break me then, I won't let it break me now.

CHAPTER 36

If he wants me, he will have to earn me.

I will not be an easy handout. I will not offer myself at no cost or come without condition. I will be worth every penny I charge, every bit of time I ask for, and every level of effort I require to a man who's looking for a woman to settle down with. I will set the bar for him just as high as the one I have set and met for myself. I am sure of who I am, and if I am to be his, he will have to show and prove to me why before he's given that privilege every single day.

CHAPTER 37

I deserve to be spoiled.

For all that I've sacrificed and for the time I've waited patiently for the things I've longed for, I deserve to experience an abundance of my heart's desires. Not just materialistically, but I deserve to be spoiled with love, time, consideration, creativity, and more. I deserve to have a man who will not stop at the bare minimum when it comes to loving me. I deserve one who looks after me and knows how to allow me to have his back as well. While I'm still preparing, I'm currently deserving of being spoiled to the fullest extent, and I will not be convinced otherwise.

CHAPTER 38

My body is beautiful, but I am so much more.

I don't have to distance myself from my flesh to know that it does not define me one way or the other. Whether society unanimously agrees that I meet their superficial standard or misses the gift that is my beauty because it doesn't come wrapped in the package they determined was the standard, I am so much more than my body. I am the thoughts that come out of nowhere in the middle of the day, the empathy I have for the less fortunate, the fight I have for the defenseless, the care I extend for my loved ones, and the perseverance I use to keep obstacles from stopping me. My body is only half the story; my other half is just as amazing.

CHAPTER 39

I will attract a man who will desire me and only me.

With all of the beautiful women this world has to offer, I'm set apart in ways my soul mate will need no convincing of. He will show that he recognizes this, not only in his actions but in the changes that take place within him for my best interests. I will not have to question who his love or lust belongs to because it will be blatantly obvious on a daily basis in the way he treats and respects me.

CHAPTER 40

No matter how deserving the retaliation, I will reserve my energy.

I will treat my energy like the temple it is, letting nothing destructive in and applying it outwardly in the same regard. I will not allow room in my heart for hate or anything that resembles it. I will speak life into those with space for it and pray for those who don't. But I will not invest myself into fruitless battles that don't help me win the war of being a better woman. I will only give my energy to things and people who give me growth in return.

CHAPTER 41

I was built to handle everything thrown my way.

Nobody said the weapon wouldn't be formed. No one told me the road would be easy. So I will not fix mine to expect what is easy, but rather remember that even when it's not, I will be just fine. I was not designed to come here and crumble. I was designed come here and conquer so that is exactly what I will do.

CHAPTER 42

I do not fear real love.

Iknow the possibility of being fooled again. I know the chances that it will all add up to nothing but wasted time and memories that last longer than the relationship. But, I refuse to allow that to stop me from going forward, giving myself another chance to be loved, correctly this time. Not all men are bad, and the right one will find me if I keep myself in position to be found. That position is nowhere near fear, therefore, fear will not be tolerated.

CHAPTER 43

My thoughts and feelings are valuable.

I know that what I have to say matters, and I recognize my potential to change a person's day, if not life, with just a few simple words. Whether I'm in a good mood or not, my feelings at any moment are valid. It doesn't matter how many or who sees value in them, they are significant and deserve to be respected. I will continue to surround myself with those who feel the same.

CHAPTER 44

I accept the possibility that someone better than I ever knew existed.

I will be the restoration for my future husband's hope in real love, and he will be mine. I will be proof to my future husband that amazing women exist, and he will be mine that great men also exist. Even if I don't see it coming, I will be open to new beginnings with someone better instead of holding on to a past for which I only settled.

CHAPTER 45

I will focus on me for as long as I need to before focusing on someone else.

If it's time I need, I'll allow myself that. If it's being in complete silence daily that I want, I will allow myself that as well. If it's traveling, splurging, or just enjoying time not being responsible for another heart that I'm longing for, I will give that to myself. I deserve a moment to focus on me until I decide it's time to let someone else focus on me for a change.

CHAPTER 46

I will have a husband who won't stop until I'm the happiest woman on Earth.

My future husband will pour his love into me until I runneth over. I won't have to beg him to try or listen to excuses of why he doesn't. I will consistently find myself thanking God for blessing me with a man with such a kind heart, full of love that belongs to me.

CHAPTER 47

I will recognize when my time is being wasted, and stop it immediately.

My time will be allotted for those who value it, not for those who squander it. Conversations that lead nowhere, gossip, nor negativity will be rewarded with my precious time. Accepting excuses that repeat themselves will not be tolerated. I will surround myself with constructive influences that leave me feeling renewed, not used.

CHAPTER 48

I am rich in happiness.

I do not need wealth to be happy. I will create it now so that it doesn't sway depending on financial circumstances one way or the other. I'll appreciate those things that matter most while I still have them and look in the mirror at what God has created when I'm in need of happiness. I won't look to my bank account. There is an abundance of things to be happy about whether it's things I have or things I've been kept away from. Happiness is all around me.

CHAPTER 49

My standards are not too high.

I will not listen to small minds tell me that I'm thinking unrealistically for wanting a love that's well within the capacity of a good man. I look forward to spending the rest of my life mentally and physically stimulated, physically and financially supported, while growing personally with a man who is doing the same.

CHAPTER 50

I will have a man who supports my dreams.

I will get up every day excited about my dreams to see he's just as excited for me. I will work hard day in and day out, and he will wait patiently to hear me vent about it. I will stay up late nights, and he will wake up to ask me if there's anything I need. I will be nervous when it's time to put my work on display, and he will be my biggest cheerleader to help me feel confident again. I will have a man who's supportive of my dreams as he works towards his own.

Chapter 51

I am a better judge of character than I've ever been.

I've made many errors in my discernment before, and it's only grown me into the best judge of character I've ever been. The snakes will not survive around me and the leeches will be revealed quicker than ever before. I will not invest years trying to change someone who doesn't want to be changed, but rather cut my ties so I can be found by a man who's ready to love right now. I will see him, recognize him, and reciprocate his love.

CHAPTER 52

I deserve the very best a man has to offer.

Despite what he may have been through, my soul mate will love me with a renewed heart and clean slate. He will come with his emotional scars the way I will, but will have also healed enough to be healthy for a relationship the way I have also. He will give me his love to me freely and abundantly. We will be an example of how to love after having love lost before. We'll be grateful we didn't give up on finding each other.

CHAPTER 53

I forgive myself.

I forgive myself for hurting others and myself. I forgive myself for falling for potential instead of their reality. I forgive myself for losing myself in their lust and wishing it would turn into love. I forgive myself for tolerating their lies and false promises when deep down, I knew it wasn't true. I forgive myself for seeing the best in them when they only gave me the worst they had to offer. I forgive myself for giving multiple chances they didn't deserve. I forgive myself for taking them back when they brought nothing new. I forgive myself for looking like a fool. I forgive myself, because I have grown and learned from that time in my life and I'm ready to move forward unapologetically.

CHAPTER 54

I am a blessing to all who come in contact with me.

My energy is radiant like the sun, and my smile shines even brighter. My words provide comfort to those who've been torn down by the messages of society. I am a place of peace for those experiencing turmoil, and I provide clarity to those who can't seem to see clearly through their circumstances. I am valuable. Those who come in to contact with me are better people as a result of it.

CHAPTER 55

I am easy to love despite those who haven't.

I give everyone multiple reasons to both love and like me as a person. My personality is not for everybody, but my love is until they prove otherwise. I may be misunderstood, but there is beauty in my complexity that the right man will appreciate me even more for. He will love me effortlessly while showing it with effort every single day the way I do for myself.

CHAPTER 56

I am worth more than just sex.

Whether I have accepted the condition in the past or not, I am worth much more than sex. I am someone to learn from and laugh with. I'm loyal. I'm growing into a better version of myself daily, and I'm able to accept correction when I'm wrong, so long as it comes from a place of love. I'm able to correct those around me from a place of love so that they make better decisions. I'm intelligent. I can endure much more than anyone can possibly throw at me. I have enough love for myself, future husband, and our children. He will get to know me and realize that sex with me would be great, but a life with me will be the real blessing.

CHAPTER 57

My worth is not determined by anyone's inability to see it.

I tried to measure myself by those equipped with broken measuring sticks in the past, but never again. I will measure myself from now on and anyone who intends to love me can only do so if they come to the same conclusion I have, that I'm worth more than any diamond or precious metal known to man. I am wonderfully made just the way I was intended. Inside and out, I am beautiful. I will not let anyone tell me otherwise, nor will I entertain anyone who tries to. I know the truth, and those who are lucky enough to stay in my life will know and show it too.

CHAPTER 58

I will not judge myself by my perception of others.

Things as I see them are not always as they appear, so I will not let delusions be the standard for which I hold myself. I will not be unrealistic in my expectations of myself, nor will I expend valuable time and energy looking to see what others are doing when my own life warrants as much of me as possible. I am on my own path, and though I may want similar destinations to others, the time it'll take for me to get there and the directions I have to go will be different. I accept and embrace that as the truth, and I am grateful for it.

CHAPTER 59

I will love the man who is for me, but I will not lose myself in the effort to do so.

I love myself because I'm worthy of it. I'm waiting for my future husband because what we will have together will be worthy of the time it takes to get to it. I am finding myself now so that there is no chance of me losing myself later in loving someone else. I have confidence in who I am and faith that my future husband will not require me to lessen myself in pursuit of him but will build me up as we pursue each other. We will not attempt to compensate for missing pieces of each other, but rather add to each other instead.

CHAPTER 60

I don't ask for much, but I deserve the best.

I may not make many requests, but those I do make are significant and meaningful. I'm deserving of the desires of my heart, and if they are truly for me, I will receive them. I have experienced the feeling of asking for too much, but I now know the problem was not with how much I was asking, but rather who I was asking for it from. For the man who will one day earn me, I will give him so much, he'll gladly give me all of him in return, and it will include everything I've ever wanted. Even without me verbalizing my needs, he will see to them consistently and work tirelessly for those he can't satisfy at the moment. He will not give me what's left of him, but rather the best of him because he will realize that I'm worth it the same way I have.

THE END

Thank you for reading. If you enjoyed this, please let us and your friends know with an honest review or via any of my official social media handles listed below.

Facebook: https://www.facebook.com/officialderrickjaxn

Instagram: https://www.instagram.com/derrickjaxn